Mountain Songs

Selections from the Psalms

Copyright © 1980 Forlaget Scandinavia Copenhagen, Denmark

Published by
Lion Publishing
Icknield Way, Tring, Herts, England
ISBN 0 85648 292 7

Albatross Books
P.O. Box 320, Sutherland, NSW 2232, Australia
ISBN 0 86760 206 6

First edition 1980

Printed by Werner Söderström Osakeyhtiö, Finland

Mountain Songs

Selections from the Psalms

Edited by
Jørgen Vium Olesen

A LION BOOK

Happy Are Those

Happy are those who reject the advice of evil men,
who do not follow the example of sinners
or join those who have no use for God.
Instead, they find joy in obeying the Law of the Lord,
and they study it day and night.
They are like trees that grow beside a stream,
that bear fruit at the right time,
and whose leaves do not dry up.
They succeed in everything they do.

But evil men are not like this at all;
they are like straw that the wind blows away.
Sinners will be condemned by God
and kept apart from God's own people.
The righteous are guided and protected by the Lord,
but the evil are on the way to their doom.

The Lord Reigns

Why do the nations plan rebellion?
Why do people make their useless plots?
Their kings revolt,
their rulers plot together against the Lord
and against the king he chose.
'Let us free ourselves from their rule,' they say;
'let us throw off their control.'

From his throne in heaven the Lord laughs
and mocks their feeble plans.
Then he warns them in anger
and terrifies them with his fury.
'On Zion, my sacred hill,' he says,
'I have installed my king.'

Ask, and I Will Give You

'I will announce,' says the king,
'what the Lord has declared.
He said to me: "You are my son;
today I have become your father.
Ask, and I will give you all the nations;
the whole earth will be yours.
You will break them with an iron rod;
you will shatter them in pieces like a clay pot." '

Now listen to this warning, you kings;
learn this lesson, you rulers of the world:
Serve the Lord with fear;
tremble and bow down to him;
or else his anger will be quickly aroused,
and you will suddenly die.
Happy are all who go to him for protection.

I Am Not Afraid

I have so many enemies, Lord,
so many who turn against me!
They talk about me and say, 'God will not help him.'

But you, O Lord, are always my shield from danger;
you give me victory and restore my courage.
I call to the Lord for help,
and from his sacred hill he answers me.

I lie down and sleep,
and all night long the Lord protects me.
I am not afraid of the thousands of enemies
who surround me on every side.

Come, Lord! Save me, my God!
You punish all my enemies
and leave them powerless to harm me.
Victory comes from the Lord—
may he bless his people.

He Hears Me

Answer me when I pray, O God, my defender!
When I was in trouble, you helped me.
Be kind to me now and hear my prayer.

How long will you people insult me?
How long will you love what is worthless
and go after what is false?

Remember that the Lord has chosen
the righteous for his own,
and he hears me when I call to him.

Tremble with fear and stop sinning;
think deeply about this,
when you lie in silence on your beds.
Offer the right sacrifices to the Lord,
and put your trust in him.

There are many who pray:
'Give us more blessings, O Lord.
Look on us with kindness!'
But the joy that you have given me
is more than they will ever have
with all their corn and wine.

When I lie down, I go to sleep in peace;
you alone, O Lord, keep me perfectly safe.

From PSALM 5

Voice in the Morning

Listen to my words, O Lord, and hear my sighs.
Listen to my cry for help, my God and king!

I pray to you, O Lord;
you hear my voice in the morning;
at sunrise I offer my prayer and wait for your answer.

You are not a God who is pleased with wrongdoing;
you allow no evil in your presence.
You cannot stand the sight of proud men;
you hate all wicked people.
You destroy all liars
and despise violent, deceitful men.

But because of your great love
I can come into your house;
I can worship in your holy Temple
and bow down to you in reverence.

Sing for Joy

Lord, I have so many enemies!
Lead me to do your will;
make your way plain for me to follow.

What my enemies say can never be trusted;
they only want to destroy.
Their words are flattering and smooth,
but full of deadly deceit.
Condemn and punish them, O God;
may their own plots cause their ruin.
Drive them out of your presence
because of their many sins
and their rebellion against you.

But all who find safety in you will rejoice;
they can always sing for joy.
Protect those who love you;
because of you they are truly happy.
You bless those who obey you, Lord;
your love protects them like a shield.

They are
like trees that
grow beside a
stream, that
bear fruit
at the right
time,
and whose
leaves do not
dry up.
They
succeed in
everything
they do.

Rescue Me from Death

Lord, don't be angry and rebuke me!
Don't punish me in your anger!
I am worn out, O Lord; have pity on me!
Give me strength; I am completely exhausted
and my whole being is deeply troubled.
How long, O Lord, will you wait to help me?
Come and save me, Lord;
in your mercy rescue me from death.
In the world of the dead you are not remembered;
no one can praise you there.

I am worn out with grief;
every night my bed is damp from my weeping;
my pillow is soaked with tears.
I can hardly see; my eyes are so swollen
from the weeping caused by my enemies.

Keep away from me, you evil men!
The Lord hears my weeping;
he listens to my cry for help
and will answer my prayer.
My enemies will know the bitter shame of defeat;
in sudden confusion they will be driven away.

God, My Protector

O Lord, my God, I come to you for protection;
rescue me and save me from all who pursue me,
or else like a lion they will carry me off
where no one can save me,
and there they will tear me to pieces.

O Lord, my God, if I have wronged anyone,
if I have betrayed a friend
or shown mercy to someone who
wronged me unjustly—
if I have done any of these things—
then let my enemies pursue me and catch me,
let them cut me down and kill me
and leave me lifeless on the ground!

Rise in your anger, O Lord!
Stand up against the fury of my enemies;
rouse yourself and help me!
Justice is what you demand,
so bring together all the peoples round you,
and rule over them from above.
You are the judge of all mankind.
Judge in my favour, O Lord;
you know that I am innocent.
You are a righteous God
and judge our thoughts and desires.
Stop the wickedness of evil men
and reward those who are good.

Consequences of Evil

God is my protector; he saves those who obey him.
God is a righteous judge
and always condemns the wicked.
If they do not change their ways,
God will sharpen his sword.
He bends his bow and makes it ready;
he takes up his deadly weapons
and aims his burning arrows.

See how wicked people think up evil;
they plan trouble and practise deception.
But in the traps they set for others,
they themselves get caught.
So they are punished by their own evil
and are hurt by their own violence.

I thank the Lord for his justice,
I sing praises to the Lord, the Most High.

Children's Song

O Lord, our Lord,
your greatness is seen in all the world!
Your praise reaches up to the heavens;
it is sung by children and babies.
You are safe and secure from all your enemies;
you stop anyone who opposes you.

When I look at the sky, which you have made,
at the moon and the stars,
which you set in their places—
what is man, that you think of him;
mere man, that you care for him?

Yet you made him inferior only to yourself;
you crowned him with glory and honour.
You appointed him ruler over everything you made;
you placed him over all creation:
sheep and cattle, and the wild animals too;
the birds and the fish and the creatures in the seas.

O Lord, our Lord,
your greatness is seen in all the world!

From PSALM 9

Tell of Wonderful Things

I will praise you, Lord, with all my heart;
I will tell of all the wonderful things you have done.
I will sing with joy because of you.
I will sing praise to you, Almighty God.

My enemies turn back when you appear;
they fall down and die.
You are fair and honest in your judgements,
and you have judged in my favour.

You have condemned the heathen
and destroyed the wicked;
they will be remembered no more.
Our enemies are finished for ever;
you have destroyed their cities,
and they are completely forgotten.

But the Lord is king for ever;
he has set up his throne for judgement.
He rules the world with righteousness;
he judges the nations with justice.

The Lord is a refuge for the oppressed,
a place of safety in times of trouble.
Those who know you, Lord, will trust you;
you do not abandon anyone who comes to you.

From PSALM 9

God Does Not Forget

Sing praise to the Lord, who rules in Zion!
Tell every nation what he has done!
God remembers those who suffer;
he does not forget their cry,
and he punishes those who wrong them.

Be merciful to me, O Lord!
See the sufferings my enemies cause me!
Rescue me from death, O Lord,
that I may stand before the people of Jerusalem
and tell them all the things for which I praise you.
I will rejoice because you saved me.

The heathen have dug a pit and fallen in;
they have been caught in their own trap.
The Lord has revealed himself
by his righteous judgements,
and the wicked are trapped by their own deeds.

Death is the destiny of all the wicked,
of all those who reject God.
The needy will not always be neglected;
the hope of the poor will not be crushed for ever.

Come, Lord! Do not let men defy you!
Bring the heathen before you
and pronounce judgement on them.
Make them afraid, O Lord;
make them know that they are only mortal beings.

In Times of Trouble

Why are you so far away, O Lord?
Why do you hide yourself when we are in trouble?
The wicked are proud and persecute the poor;
catch them in the traps they have made.

The wicked man is proud of his evil desires;
the greedy man curses and rejects the Lord.
A wicked man does not care about the Lord;
in his pride he thinks that God doesn't matter.

A wicked man succeeds in everything.
He cannot understand God's judgements;
he sneers at his enemies.
He says to himself, 'I will never fail;
I will never be in trouble.'
His speech is filled with curses, lies, and threats;
he is quick to speak hateful, evil words.

He hides himself in the villages,
waiting to murder innocent people.
He spies on his helpless victims;
he waits in his hiding place like a lion.
He lies in wait for the poor;
he catches them in his trap and drags them away.

The helpless victims lie crushed;
brute strength has defeated them.
The wicked man says to himself, 'God doesn't care!
He has closed his eyes and will never see me!'

When I look at
the sky, which you have made,
at the moon and the stars, which you
set in their places—what is man,
that you think of him; mere man,
that you care for him?

Those with Needs

O Lord, punish those wicked men!
Remember those who are suffering!
How can a wicked man despise God
and say to himself, 'He will not punish me'?

But you do see; you take notice of trouble
and suffering and are always ready to help.
The helpless man commits himself to you;
you have always helped the needy.

Break the power of wicked and evil men;
punish them for the wrong they have done
until they do it no more.

The Lord is king for ever and ever.
Those who worship other gods
will vanish from his land.

You will listen, O Lord, to the prayers of the lowly;
you will give them courage.
You will hear the cries of the oppressed
and the orphans; you will judge in their favour,
so that mortal men may cause terror no more.

Safety

I trust in the Lord for safety.
How foolish of you to say to me,
'Fly away like a bird to the mountains,
because the wicked have drawn their bows
and aimed their arrows
to shoot at good men in the darkness.
There is nothing a good man can do
when everything falls apart.'

The Lord is in his holy temple;
he has his throne in heaven.
He watches people everywhere
and knows what they are doing.
He examines the good and the wicked alike;
the lawless he hates with all his heart.

He sends down flaming coals and
burning sulphur on the wicked;
he punishes them with scorching winds.
The Lord is righteous and loves good deeds;
those who do them will live in his presence.

The Promises of God

Help us, Lord!
There is not a good man left;
honest men can no longer be found.
All of them lie to one another;
they deceive each other with flattery.

Silence those flattering tongues, O Lord!
Close those boastful mouths that say,
'With our words we get what we want.
We will say what we wish, and no one can stop us.'

'But now I will come,' says the Lord,
'because the needy are oppressed
and the persecuted groan in pain.
I will give them the security they long for.'

The promises of the Lord can be trusted;
they are as genuine as silver
refined seven times in the furnace.

Wicked men are everywhere,
and everyone praises what is evil.
Keep us always safe, O Lord,
and preserve us from such people.

When God Hides Himself

How much longer will you forget me, Lord? For ever?
How much longer will you hide yourself from me?
How long must I endure trouble?
How long will sorrow fill my heart day and night?
How long will my enemies triumph over me?

Look at me, O Lord my God, and answer me.
Restore my strength; don't let me die.
Don't let my enemies say, 'We have defeated him.'
Don't let them gloat over my downfall.

I rely on your constant love;
I will be glad, because you will rescue me.
I will sing to you, O Lord,
because you have been good to me.

Expectations

Fools say to themselves, 'There is no God.'
They are all corrupt,
and they have done terrible things;
there is no one who does what is right.

The Lord looks down from heaven at mankind
to see if there are any who are wise,
any who worship him.
But they have all gone wrong;
they are all equally bad.
Not one of them does what is right,
not a single one.

'Don't they know?' asks the Lord.
'Are all these evildoers ignorant?
They live by robbing my people,
and they never pray to me.'

But then they will be terrified,
for God is with those who obey him.
Evildoers frustrate the plans of the humble man,
but the Lord is his protection.

How I pray that victory will come to Israel from Zion.
How happy the people of Israel will be
when the Lord makes them prosperous again!

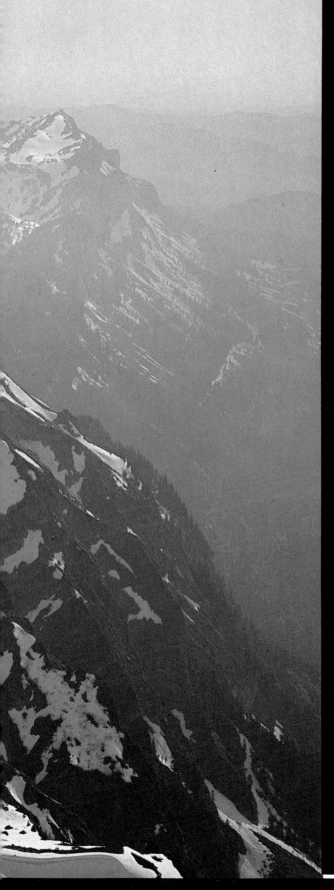

Entering God's Presence

Lord, who may enter your Temple?
Who may worship on Zion, your sacred hill?

A person who obeys God in everything
and always does what is right,
whose words are true and sincere,
and who does not slander others.
He does no wrong to his friends
and does not spread rumours about his neighbours.
He despises those whom God rejects,
but honours those who obey the Lord.
He always does what he promises,
no matter how much it may cost.
He makes loans without charging interest
and cannot be bribed to testify against the innocent.

Whoever does these things will always be secure.

All I Need

Protect me, O God; I trust in you for safety.
I say to the Lord, 'You are my Lord;
all the good things I have come from you.'

How excellent are the Lord's faithful people!
My greatest pleasure is to be with them.

Those who rush to other gods
bring many troubles on themselves.
I will not take part in their sacrifices;
I will not worship their gods.

You, Lord, are all I have,
and you give me all I need;
my future is in your hands.
How wonderful are your gifts to me;
how good they are!

I praise the Lord, because he guides me,
and in the night my conscience warns me.

I am always
aware of the Lord's presence;
he is near, and nothing
can shake me.

53

Joy in His Presence

I am always aware of the Lord's presence;
he is near, and nothing can shake me.

And so I am thankful and glad,
and I feel completely secure,
because you protect me from the power of death,
and the one you love you will not
abandon to the world of the dead.

You will show me the path that leads to life;
your presence fills me with joy
and brings me pleasure for ever.

God's Way

Listen, O Lord, to my plea for justice;
pay attention to my cry for help!
Listen to my honest prayer.
You will judge in my favour,
because you know what is right.

You know my heart.
You have come to me at night;
you have examined me completely
and found no evil desire in me.
I speak no evil as others do;
I have obeyed your command
and have not followed paths of violence.
I have always walked in your way
and have never strayed from it.

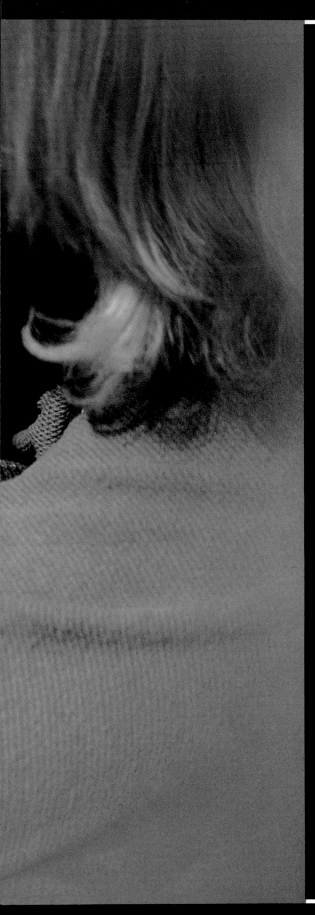

Wonderful Love

I pray to you, O God, because you answer me;
so turn to me and listen to my words.
Reveal your wonderful love and save us;
at your side we are safe from our enemies.

Protect me as you would your very eyes;
hide me in the shadow of your wings
from the attacks of the wicked.

Deadly enemies surround me;
they have no pity and speak proudly.
They are round me now, wherever I turn,
watching for a chance to pull me down.
They are like lions, waiting for me,
wanting to tear me to pieces.
Come, Lord! Oppose my enemies and defeat them!
Save me from the wicked by your sword;
save me from those who in this life have all they want.
Punish them with the sufferings you
have stored up for them;
may there be enough for their children
and some left over for their children's children!

But I will see you, because I have done no wrong;
and when I awake, your presence will fill me with joy.

Safe from Enemies

How I love you, Lord! You are my defender.

The Lord is my protector; he is my strong fortress.
My God is my protection, and with him I am safe.
He protects me like a shield;
he defends me and keeps me safe.
I call to the Lord,
and he saves me from my enemies.
Praise the Lord!

Majesty of God

The danger of death was all round me;
the waves of destruction rolled over me.
The danger of death was round me,
and the grave set its trap for me.
In my trouble I called to the Lord;
I called to my God for help.
In his temple he heard my voice;
he listened to my cry for help.

Then the earth trembled and shook;
the foundations of the mountains
rocked and quivered, because God was angry.
Smoke poured out of his nostrils,
a consuming flame and burning coals from his mouth.
He tore the sky apart and came down
with a dark cloud under his feet.
He flew swiftly on a winged creature;
he travelled on the wings of the wind.
He covered himself with darkness;
thick clouds, full of water, surrounded him.
Hailstones and flashes of fire
came from the lightning before him
and broke through the dark clouds.

Rescue in Trouble

Then the Lord thundered from the sky;
and the voice of the Most High was heard.
He shot his arrows and scattered his enemies;
with flashes of lightning he sent them running.
The floor of the ocean was laid bare,
and the foundations of the earth were uncovered,
when you rebuked your enemies, Lord,
and roared at them in anger.

The Lord reached down from above
and took hold of me;
he pulled me out of the deep waters.
He rescued me from my powerful enemies
and from all those who hate me—
they were too strong for me.
When I was in trouble, they attacked me,
but the Lord protected me.
He helped me out of danger;
he saved me because he was pleased with me.

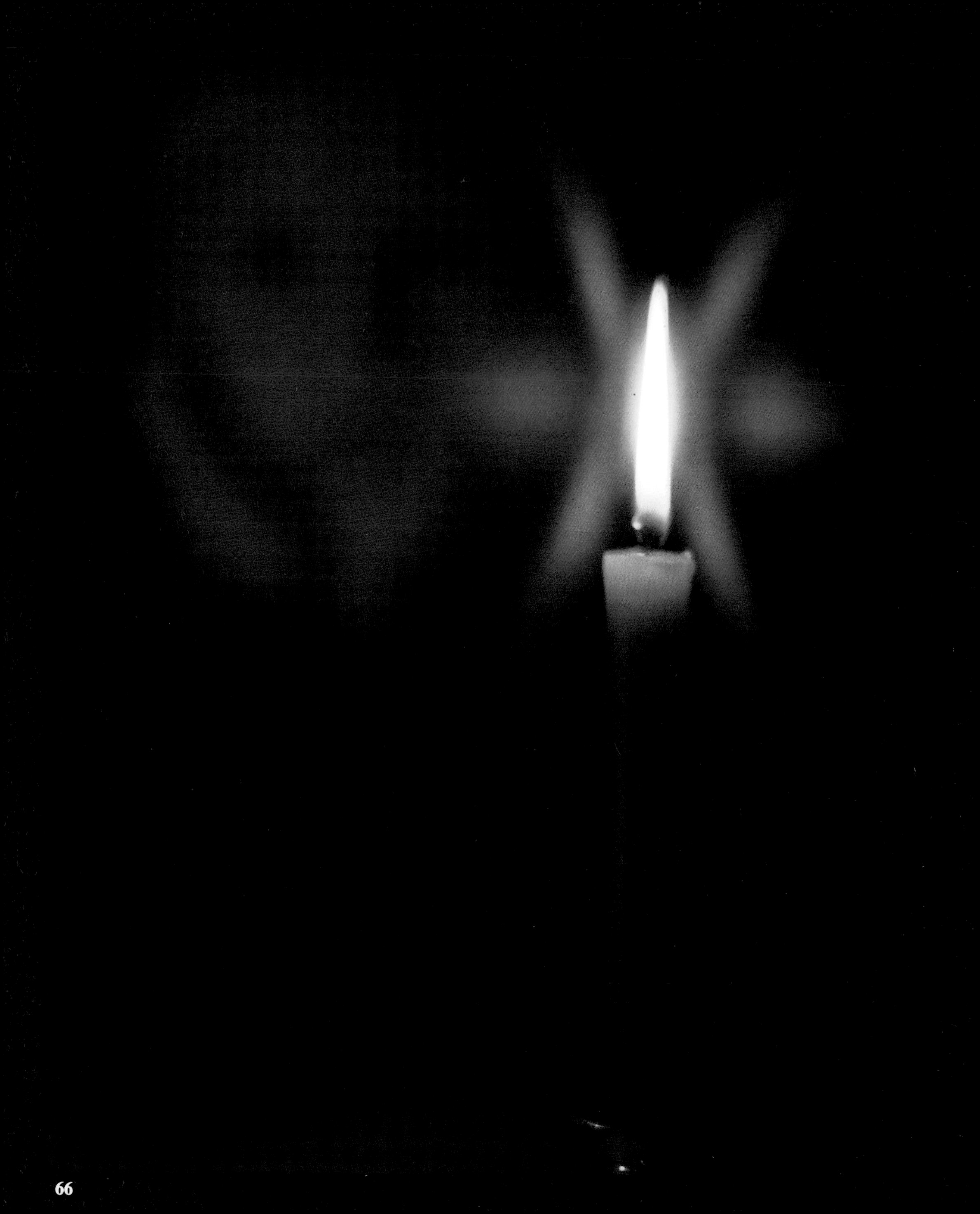

From PSALM 18

Light in Darkness

The Lord rewards me because I do what is right;
he blesses me because I am innocent.
I have obeyed the law of the Lord;
I have not turned away from my God.
I have observed all his laws;
I have not disobeyed his commands.
He knows that I am faultless,
that I have kept myself from doing wrong.
And so he rewards me because I do what is right,
because he knows that I am innocent.

O Lord, you are faithful to those who
are faithful to you;
completely good to those who are perfect.
You are pure to those who are pure,
but hostile to those who are wicked.
You save those who are humble,
but you humble those who are proud.

O Lord, you give me light;
you dispel my darkness.
You give me strength to attack my enemies
and power to overcome their defences.

*O Lord, our Lord,
your greatness is seen
in all the world!*

From PSALM 18

Foothold on the Mountains

This God — how perfect are his deeds!
How dependable his words!
He is like a shield for all who seek his protection.
The Lord alone is God; God alone is our defence.
He is the God who makes me strong,
who makes my pathway safe.
He makes me sure-footed as a deer;
he keeps me safe on the mountains.
He trains me for battle,
so that I can use the strongest bow.

O Lord, you protect me and save me;
your care has made me great,
and your power has kept me safe.
You have kept me from being captured,
and I have never fallen.
I pursue my enemies and catch them;
I do not stop until I destroy them.
I strike them down, and they cannot rise;
they lie defeated before me.
You give me strength for the battle
and victory over my enemies.
You make my enemies run from me;
I destroy those who hate me.
They cry for help, but no one saves them;
they call to the Lord, but he does not answer.
I crush them, so that they become like dust
which the wind blows away.
I trample on them like mud in the streets.

The Lord Lives!

You saved me from a rebellious people
and made me ruler over the nations;
people I did not know have now become my subjects.
Foreigners bow before me;
when they hear me, they obey.
They lose their courage
and come trembling from their fortresses.

The Lord lives! Praise my defender!
Proclaim the greatness of the God who saves me.
He gives me victory over my enemies;
he subdues the nations under me
and saves me from my foes.

O Lord, you give me victory over my enemies
and protect me from violent men.
And so I praise you among the nations;
I sing praises to you.

God gives great victories to his king;
he shows constant love to the one he has chosen,
to David and his descendants for ever.

God's Glory in Creation

How clearly the sky reveals God's glory!
How plainly it shows what he has done!
Each day announces it to the following day;
each night repeats it to the next.
No speech or words are used, no sound is heard;
yet their voice goes out to all the world
and is heard to the ends of the earth.
God made a home in the sky for the sun;
it comes out in the morning like a happy bridegroom,
like an athlete eager to run a race.
It starts at one end of the sky
and goes across to the other.
Nothing can hide from its heat.

I will praise you, Lord, with all my heart; I will tell of all the wonderful things you have done. I will sing because of you. I will sing praise to you, Almighty God.